THE
VIRGO
ORACLE

THE
VIRGO
ORACLE

INSTANT ANSWERS FROM
YOUR COSMIC SELF

STELLA FONTAINE

greenfinch

Introduction

Welcome to your zodiac oracle,
carefully crafted especially for you
Virgo, and brimming with the
wisdom of the universe.

Is there a tricky-to-answer question niggling at you and you need an answer?

Whenever you're unsure whether to say 'yes' or 'no', whether to go back or to carry on, whether to trust or to turn away, make some time for a personal session with your very own oracle. Drawing on your astrological profile, your zodiac oracle will guide you in understanding, interpreting and answering those burning questions that life throws your way. Discovering your true path will become an enlightening journey of self-actualization.

Humans have long cast their eyes heavenwards to seek answers from the universe. For millennia the sun, moon and stars have been our constant companions as they repeat their paths and patterns across the skies. We continue to turn to the cosmos for guidance, trusting in the deep and abiding wisdom of the universe as we strive for fulfilment, truth and understanding.

The most basic and familiar aspect of astrology draws on the twelve signs of the zodiac, each connected to a unique constellation as well as its own particular colours, numbers and characteristics. These twelve familiar signs are also known as the sun signs: Aries, Taurus, Gemini, Cancer, Leo, Virgo, Libra, Scorpio, Sagittarius, Capricorn, Aquarius and Pisces.

Aries   Taurus   Gemini   Cancer   Leo   Virgo

Libra   Scorpio   Sagittarius   Capricorn   Aquarius   Pisces

Each sign is associated with an element (fire, air, earth or water), and also carries a particular quality: cardinal (action-takers), fixed (steady and constant) and mutable (changeable and transformational). Beginning to understand these complex combinations, and to recognize the layered influences they bring to bear on your life, will unlock your own potential for personal insight, self-awareness and discovery.

In our data-flooded lives, now more than ever it can be difficult to know where to turn for guidance and advice. With your astrology oracle always by your side, navigating life's twists and turns will become a smoother, more mindful process. Harness the prescience of the stars and tune in to the resonance of your sun sign with this wisdom-packed guide that will lead you to greater self-knowledge and deeper confidence in the decisions you are making. Of course, not all questions are created equal; your unique character, your circumstances and the issues with which you find yourself confronted all add up to a conundrum unlike any other... but with your question in mind and your zodiac oracle in your hand, you're already halfway to the answer.

Virgo
AUGUST 23 TO SEPTEMBER 22

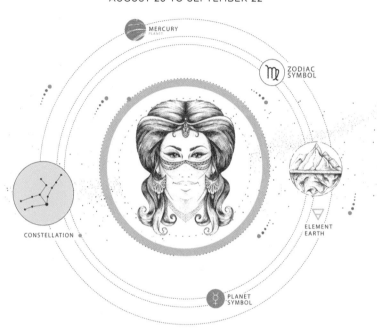

MERCURY
PLANET

ZODIAC
SYMBOL

CONSTELLATION

ELEMENT
EARTH

PLANET
SYMBOL

Element: Earth

Quality: Mutable

Named for the constellation: Virgo (the virgin)

Ruled by: Mercury

Opposite: Pisces

Characterized by: Loyalty, creativity, practicality

Colour: Yellow, greys

How to Use This Book

You can engage with your oracle whenever you need to but, for best results, create an atmosphere of calm and quiet, somewhere you will not be disturbed, making a place for yourself and your question to take priority. Whether this is a particular physical area you turn to in times of contemplation, or whether you need to fence off a dedicated space within yourself during your busy day, that all depends on you and your circumstances. Whichever you choose, it is essential that you actively put other thoughts and distractions to one side in order to concentrate upon the question you wish to answer.

Find a comfortable position, cradle this book lightly in your hands, close your eyes, centre yourself. Focus on the question you wish to ask. Set your intention gently and mindfully towards your desire to answer this question, to the exclusion of all other thoughts and mind-chatter. Allow all else to float softly away, as you remain quiet and still, gently watching the shape and form of the question you wish to address. Gently deepen and slow your breathing.

Tune in to the ancient resonance of your star sign, the vibrations of your surroundings, the beat of your heart and the flow of life and the universe moving in and around you. You are one with the universe.

Now simply press the book between your palms as you clearly and distinctly ask your question (whether aloud or in your head), then open it at any page. Open your eyes. Your advice will be revealed.

Read it carefully. Take your time turning this wisdom over in your mind, allowing your thoughts to surround it, to absorb it, flow with it, then to linger and settle where they will.

Remember, your oracle will not provide anything as blunt and brutal as a completely literal answer. That is not its role. Rather, you will be gently guided towards the truth you seek through your own consciousness, experience and understanding. And as a result, you will grow, learn and flourish.

Let's begin.

Close your eyes.

Hold the question you want
answered clearly in your mind.

Open your oracle to any page to
reveal your cosmic insight.

Mercury, your ruling planet, has gifted you with a particular love and affinity for communication and travel. The two sit very well together and, as you've been a bit stuck for a while now, how about planning your next trip?

Working with a team is not always your favourite situation, but with your gift for communication and enough time allocated to your own work, it can be a very satisfactory arrangement.

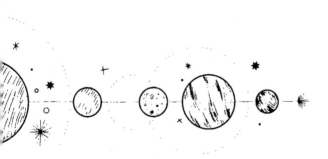

Others tend to see your Virgoan value system as unnecessarily complicated, despite how obvious and straightforward it clearly is. Pay them no attention.

True to your Virgo nature, you might be placing a little too much pressure on yourself again. This is a difficult one, but not for the obvious reasons. Take a few moments today to pause and reflect in nature, and your answer will reveal itself.

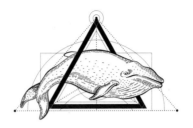

Ease off on the self-criticism
and show yourself some love. It is
said one can never step into the same
river twice. Take a deep breath and
approach this problem from a different
angle. Or look for a footbridge.

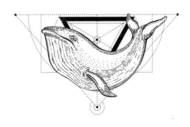

As clever and capable as you are,
sometimes you need to be patient
and wait for the world to catch up.
There is something you
still need to know.

Virgo is a mutable sign, meaning that you are adaptable, communicative and particularly adept at assisting others through transition. Use your talents wisely – change is coming.

Be mindful to include movement and activity in everything you do right now Virgo. Keep the energy flowing.

You may have surprised even yourself with a recent sudden about-face. Be gentle with yourself about it, Virgo. As you grow as a person, inevitably your ideas change, too.

If interactions with a particular person seem to inevitably result in conflict, be brave and suggest a conversation to clear the air. Whatever the result, you will have done the right thing.

Being a Virgo perfectionist,
relinquishing control can feel
unnecessarily risky. But you must
learn to trust your stars; your path
ahead is already illuminated.

Change approaches, but you do not
need to start planning yet – much as
you would love to. Try to remain open
to all the possibilities that lie ahead.

Your Virgo tendency to want to help everyone see things 'the right way' will only exhaust you on this occasion. Worry less about what other people think; you cannot control their feelings.

A sequence of small wins will be the secret to your success. Persist.

Perhaps you feel rewards aren't
flowing in the right direction Virgo.
Remind yourself that this path is not
chosen for personal gain.

With Pisces as your polar opposite sign, sometimes you need to relax your Virgo grip and go with the tidal flow. Now is one of those times.

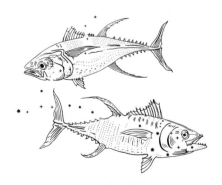

Patience and persistence provide
the best course of action right now.

Slow down and step out of the bustle today Virgo. With pressures mounting all the time, there is a danger that you will miss out on what really matters.

No ultimate rewards are
promised for endless struggle
or self-sacrifice Virgo; there is no
guarantee of a prize. Embrace chances
of happiness along the way.

Chasing impossible dreams, or trying to stitch together irreparable rifts, may simply not be worth it Virgo. Find a task more deserving of your not-inconsiderable talents.

Although your Virgo heart finds nothing as pleasurable as putting your own house in order, your full potential is not to be found in gazing inwards. Relax the self-criticism and look around you.

A deepened understanding will simplify your approach. Set aside distractions and focus on the task at hand. Time spent learning is never wasted.

Be brave. While first impressions
are treasured by every Virgo, there is a
very, very tiny chance that you might
be wrong once in a while. It is time to
allow that possibility.

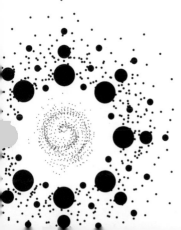

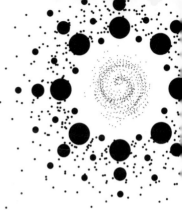

Mercury makes you a hard
worker, so it's time to make the most
of your skills. Do not shy away from
this particular challenge. Nothing
worth doing seems easy at first.

It's time to quiet your noisy, bustling Virgo thoughts and trust your gut instinct. Your first impulse was the right one.

Believe in yourself, your typical
Virgo thoughtfulness and meticulous
approach won't let you down. You
have the strength and knowledge
already within you to make the
right decision.

It may not be the easiest path,
but your intuition is already telling you
that it will take you in the direction you
are destined to travel.

Your Virgo sensitivity can sometimes trap you into a holding pattern. Uncertain times call for decisive action; pick a direction and get moving.

Keep a close eye on your capacity for jealousy and anger Virgo. Controlling your temper can feel like a full-time job some days, but it is worth it to avoid those destructive outbursts. Find smaller outlets to relieve some of the pressure.

Where is this taking you Virgo?
Now is not the time for over-thinking
but hold this little question in your
mind as you go about everything else.
The answer, when it comes, will nudge
you in the right direction.

Although your infallible
Virgoan instinct for neatness means
you tend to avoid the messiness of
out-and-out conflict, you seem to
attract more than your fair share of
sticky situations. Resist the urge to
sweep things tidily under the rug this
time; just watch and wait.

Leave the over-thinking at the door today, decide you're going to do it and just get on with it. No excuses.

You are already so well-equipped Virgo, with an unbreakable work ethic, inspired creative and problem-solving skills, and an unflagging commitment to trying to attain perfection. If anything else is missing, a quick learner like you can simply pick it up as you go along.

Step boldly forwards and meet this one whole-heartedly Virgo; there is no need or room for uncertainty. You will not look back.

When you know what it is you
really want, there is nothing more
powerful than the razor-sharp
attention to detail that Virgo is
so famous for.

It may sometimes feel like the world is against you Virgo, but breathe, and wait, and this too shall pass.

Creativity and imagination are your companions on this journey. Just don't let your Virgo tendency for over-thinking send you off course.

You can only reach for the
stars if your feet are firmly planted,
otherwise you will just be floating
about grasping desperately.
Reconsider your approach.

A little self-love will do you a lot of good Virgo, even though the idea of indulgence doesn't always sit well with you. Perhaps it might help to think of self-care as practical and essential maintenance rather than a treat?

Apply some nature tonic Virgo –
it is powerful medicine, especially
for you Earth signs. Get out there
into the green outdoors.

Anything is possible. But you might need to consider all angles. The direction of approach will make all the difference.

Of course, others can make things more difficult than they need to be – the old saying 'If you want something done properly, do it yourself' was most likely coined by a Virgo. But do try to accept help this time (if you can bear to) – it might make things that little bit easier.

Set that noisy thinking brain of yours to mute for a little while. Listen, focus, notice, feel, acknowledge, stay present.

Relinquishing control feels risky, there's no doubt about that, especially when you know others tend to take more of an easy-going approach... But on this occasion a big-picture view will be the only way to achieve a fair and balanced outcome.

Forgive others and yourself for mistakes made on life's path. You will come to understand that, ultimately, your goals were the same.

Find time for that solitude your
soul craves Virgo, either at a distance
from others or simply through
meditative activities and solitary
pursuits. Your need to recharge in this
way is not an affectation, but rather an
intrinsic part of your being. Honour it.

Time to take a break from your thinking mind. Trust your intuition to spark a few heart-connections for you.

You are kind, clever, creative, inventive and fabulous company, but only if you allow yourself enough time to rest and repair in between encounters. Take time today to recalibrate, recharge and refresh your spirit.

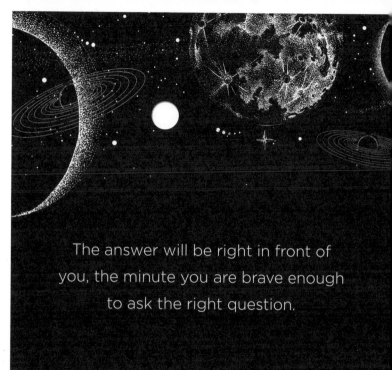

The answer will be right in front of you, the minute you are brave enough to ask the right question.

Follow your gut instinct on this one
– your first impression was correct.

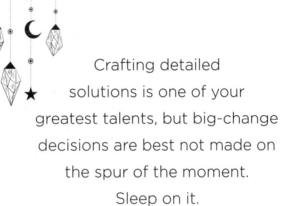

Crafting detailed
solutions is one of your
greatest talents, but big-change
decisions are best not made on
the spur of the moment.
Sleep on it.

You often feel misunderstood (what Virgo doesn't?) but remember that actions speak louder than words. You are what you do, not what you say.

If you are sensing
negativity and bad energy,
whatever form it takes, protect
yourself with a little distance. Do not
allow the fixed position of
others to limit you.

You may think you are naturally
pretty solitary Virgo, but really you
relish the opportunity to join with
others (selectively, of course) and to
develop meaningful connections. Don't
deny yourself this opportunity
– it is soul-nourishing.

Virgo, determined as you are,
you can surely see by now that this
one probably won't budge.
Stop pushing.

Even while you guard that sensitive Virgo ego, remember that a true friend is one who tells you what you need to hear, rather than simply what you want to hear. That said, there is nothing more appealing than someone who has your back.

Try to reset your impulse
to aim straight for the 'correct'
solution like a heat-seeking
missile. If you can, wait to see
what the universe offers
up in its own time.

Resist your Virgo impulse to over-think on this occasion: it will only lead you around in a self-defeating circle.

Not all obstacles have to be grappled with; it's not your first impulse, but stepping around the problem rather than becoming entangled in a big sticky mess is a more elegant solution this time.

Remember, there is a difference between friendship and flattery.

Self-doubt will not serve you well;
resist second guessing this one.

The circumstances might not be
quite as they seem – exercise your
famous Virgo caution and take
another look before you make
your decision.

Your success will depend on doing
the very thing you think you are
afraid of. Be brave Virgo!

If it feels too difficult, consider disengaging for a while. Not everyone is the same.

You are an excellent listener, often even hearing the unsaid things. But you must speak up for yourself as well, otherwise you risk being overlooked.

Resist the urge to pick a path while
emotions rule your headspace.

Your usual approach – head-down and task-oriented – may not seem to be bringing you the usual satisfaction Virgo. Perhaps there is a reason you feel distracted, something your memory is trying to bring up to the top of your consciousness...

Your love of deep immersion in your work is admirable and a big part of what makes you proud to be you. But it can also provide the most perfect excuse for isolating yourself. Stop avoiding your real life.

Don't undersell yourself, no matter your audience. What you project is what others will receive.

It is never too late for an apology.

You cannot rewrite the past,
no matter how much regret you
carry and how much you might long
to have done things differently. But
living with shame benefits no one;
your future is entirely in your hands.
Learn the lessons and move on.

The answer is right in front of you;
do the thing you are most sure you
won't regret later on. That is the
greatest wisdom you can bring
to the current situation.

Responsible and self-sacrificing,
in true Virgo style you still long for
recognition. This approach might
mean you miss out on an opportunity
now and again. Now is the time
to take a chance.

You will find a way Virgo, but it doesn't need to be the hardest path possible. Take the easier route this time.

Patience is certainly one of your
star-given virtues, but only if you can
see the promise of light at the end of
the tunnel. In many ways you're more
a sprinter than a marathon runner.
Bear in mind, different people
will do this differently.

Resist your Virgo urge to take control of the situation. Of course, you would do it best, with the most rigorous attention to detail and the closest eye on outcomes... but allow all the options this time. The right one will reveal itself soon.

Don't be too suspicious of an easy win this time; something much more difficult is just around the corner.

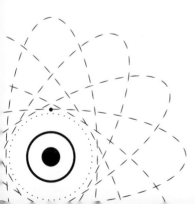

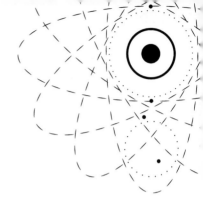

Others might call you controlling (the very idea...), but all you want to do is protect the hard work and thought you have already invested. Be careful that your Virgo instinct for caution doesn't tip over into something else.

Put your hard-working approach
to good use Virgo, and find a way to
carry on. Slowing your pace at this
point will not guarantee the
best rewards.

Secretly ambitious, definitely
hard-working and desiring of success
– that's all classic Virgo. But don't
forget that softer, more vulnerable
part, the you in you, which is
the bit that really matters.

There is a chance you are over-thinking this; be careful your attempts to correct self-consciousness or social awkwardness won't be misinterpreted as indifference or a lack of concern.

Even though it goes against all your Virgo instincts for self-preservation, sometimes you need to allow the risk of being hurt in order to give yourself a real chance. Being too cowardly to try at all will be the real failure.

Allow your talents to spread out into the opportunities presenting themselves – you have many strings to your bow Virgo, great intelligence and a varied portfolio of skills. Don't step back from an opportunity that might have been tailor-made for you.

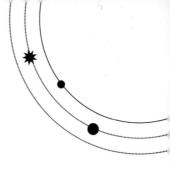

Take things slowly for the time being – even though it might feel like something must be done immediately, set your Virgo impatience aside. You will know when the time is right.

Your Virgo talents for spotting potential pitfalls and perfect planning will be in great demand. Time to look ahead and focus on the future.

Pearls of wisdom are more likely
to reveal themselves if you allow
yourself some peace and solitude.
Silence and space are imperative if
you are going to sort this one out.

Pull yourself together from the core and engage with structure, clarity and intention. Stand tall.

People come and go Virgo; the one constant in your life is you. Let your loved ones know how much they mean to you and hold yourself open to love even if it does mean you run the risk of being hurt. But do not make the mistake of allowing another person's presence, or lack thereof, to define you.

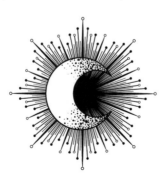

Putting on your intellectual cloak
as an excuse for disengagement is a
poor disguise Virgo; true strength
comes from humility and the
courage to be vulnerable.

Feeling inspired Virgo? When
your creativity cup runneth over, go
with it. Your problem-solving abilities
will increase massively, while your
imagination holds the key to unlocking
all that big-picture potential.

You are happiest outdoors
Virgo, and as a nature-loving
Earth sign it will rebalance you as
well. Surround yourself with plants,
indoors and out, and take the time to
simply be with the sounds, sights,
scents and sensations of nature
whenever possible.

Getting your point across
can sometimes seem the most
important thing to a Virgo. But ask
yourself whether that will really solve
this problem, or whether there are
deeper, more complicated currents
running beneath this one.

Do not allow this one to fester; you know your own nature Virgo, and if you allow this to burrow down deep into your garden of resentments it will take root and stay with you for years. See it, acknowledge it, allow it and let it go. You are not required to have a response any deeper than this – it is not your problem to carry.

Take your sunshine and small
joys anywhere you can find them.
You are entitled to them.

Accept the praise, compliments
and loving-kindness of others.
Blocking this goodwill only obstructs
your energy and it can be difficult
to start moving again. Adopt a
graceful approach and keep
on flowing through.

Do not allow your insecurities
to dominate your thoughts or
compromise your health. Allow
them, but only as part of the whole.
Concentrate instead on your strengths.

Being right might not be the only goal
worth aiming for on this occasion.
Take a more pragmatic approach.

Escapism is important in maintaining your Virgo wellbeing, especially when reality seems just that bit too real. Indulge yourself in books, travel, music and films to take a break from your everyday.

People will quickly accept your offers of help, so be sure you can really deliver without diminishing your own energies too much. If you change your mind, say so.

Accepting your responsibility to yourself can be difficult Virgo, but If you won't put yourself first then nobody else will either.

Your high Virgo standards can be exhausting, both for you and those around you. Consciously lowering your expectations of perfection will allow everyone some breathing space and you may even find you are pleasantly surprised.

Connection is one of Virgo's purest
joys – with others, with nature, with
the energy around you and of course
with yourself. You know better
than most how intoxicating
that spark can be.

Find that sweet-spot between activity and passivity Virgo – so often it eludes you and you tip too far one way or the other. Right now, it is especially important that you are equally able to speak out and listen carefully.

Insight and intuition are second nature to you Virgo, but they can at times feel like a weight rather than a gift. Remember, it is not always necessary to act on everything you know. Watch, and wait, and allow others to judge for themselves.

Check in honestly with yourself to be sure you are not sacrificing too much at the moment. Having to split your attention can sometimes feel almost physically painful, but you need to decide where your priorities really lie.

Keep a mental checklist of the things you can do to stay balanced. Remember you are an Earth sign Virgo – keep moving, swim in fresh water, enfold yourself in nature's embrace. Above all, be kind to yourself.

It can be a surprise to those around you (and sometimes to you as well) when your cutting Virgo temper flares; but you are ruled by Mercury, so of course you will see red sometimes. Retaining a measured approach and taking a step back is vital. Very rarely is an immediate, knee-jerk response required.

Leave others the space to make their own mistakes. You cannot possibly help everyone.

Bringing solutions rather than simply flagging problems is key to securing your place Virgo. No one is irreplaceable, but some are invaluable. Be one of them.

Complicated emotions will take a long while to process Virgo, and you know you like to do things properly. You can handle this, but take it slowly and be careful of yourself as you go. Ask for help if you need it.

Hurt and disappointment
usually cause a Virgo to melt into
the background for a while, retreating
like a wounded animal until the coast
is clear. But uncomfortable as it may
be, you should make the effort to
stand your ground on this one.

Subtlety is particularly beautiful to you Virgo, but you must bear in mind that it doesn't register with those who take slightly less nuanced notice of what's going on. Be sure your meaning is understood.

Others rubbing you up the
wrong way might be simply their
not-very-gentle attempts to get close
to you. Don't immediately dismiss
them because of a slightly
scratchy start.

Everything looks good next to something worse. Judge this situation on its own merits rather than by comparing.

Give others the space to speak and respect their voices, rather than taking control and dismissing their opinions because you have already made up your mind. It might take others a little longer to get to the point than it takes you, but they have something important to say so you must listen.

Making fine distinctions is a
particular Virgo skill; be sure your
communication is clear enough
that others can understand
your point and reasoning.

Virgo, you are nurturing, warm
and endlessly loyal to those you love,
but even you must admit you can
come across as a little chilly to start
with. Try to relax into this one and give
a little bit more of yourself, the
results may surprise you.

Your memory is the stuff of legend and your Virgo eye for detail means you rarely miss anything. Don't let others take this skill of yours for granted though – they should do their own hard work. You have enough on your plate.

Mind games aren't really your thing, but your Virgo style of plain speaking can sometimes catch others off-guard. Being diplomatic isn't the same as being manipulative; you're just doing others the favour of allowing them to arrive at the truth in their own time.

Impatience with others is a life-long irritation for a Virgo; others are simply not thorough, or detailed, or thoughtful, or, well, *perfect* enough. It's time to embrace the beauty in imperfection – easing your strict adherence to that self-styled rule sheet will bring you greater freedom than you can imagine.

Don't close down that hotline between your head and your intuition – it is one of the most vital tools in your Virgo-vibe basket.

Harsh or truthful? Everyone sees
this one differently.

Known for your intelligence and wisdom, combined with an analytical approach and a love of fairness, you are often the first port of call for a friend in need of advice. Be sure you bring the same level of concentration to finding solutions to your own problems.

Don't let your ego race in front of you on this one. Intoxicating as it is to feel you have it all worked out – and of course to stake your claim to the solution – you would be best advised to adopt a cautious approach.

The various pressures of work, friends, family and the energy of the day can all seem too much for you sometimes. You like focus, and love nothing more than ticking off that to-do list. Take it one thing at a time.

Others may be undecided and
more interested in talking about issues
than finding practical solutions.
Rather than feeling they are letting
you down, pay attention to the ways
that you can carry on regardless.

When you are blessed with new ideas, don't feel you need to keep them to yourself. Sharing this inspiration will increase its reach and subsequent returns many times over.

Innovation is key to keeping things fresh and continuing to feed the ideas-collection. Creativity breeds creativity Virgo – share it out and plenty will come back to you.

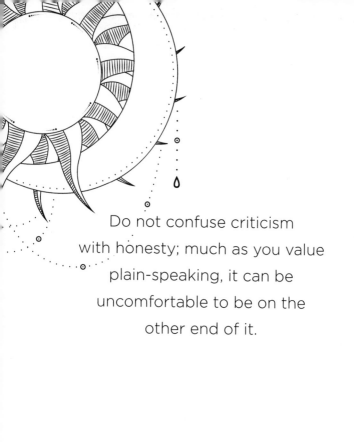

Do not confuse criticism
with honesty; much as you value
plain-speaking, it can be
uncomfortable to be on the
other end of it.

Be aware of the difference between compassion and empathy. Allowing constant empathy may saturate you in the feelings of others and ultimately exhaust your vital energies. Sometimes you need to shut the door, for your own sake.

Stay alert and keep your sensors switched on. All that hard work is about to pay off.

Allow your creativity to flow freely and follow those new ideas to see where they lead, no matter how off-the-wall they might seem at first. Others will want to help you when they catch the scent of what you're cooking up.

If you find yourself with a little more time or energy than you had anticipated, consider ploughing it into straightening out some new ways to organize yourself, your life or your belongings. A busy time lies ahead and clearing the decks before the pressure strikes will be helpful.

Try doing things in a different way this time; focus on the positives rather than the problems, be kind to yourself and remember that resilience is all about bouncing forwards cleanly into the next situation rather than feasting on the hurts of the past.

You believe that, in theory at least, a perfect world should be possible... it's just all those pesky other people who keep getting in the way. Time to embrace the imperfection, you will come to understand that, topsy-turvy as it sounds, this is where the true perfect lives. Quite a journey this, isn't it?

Do not allow the opinions and expectations of others, especially those who think they know you so well, to restrict the ways you want to move forwards into the person you wish to become. Congratulate yourself on your successes and embrace this opportunity to grow.

You have only to live your own life, no one else's. Stop casting around for comparisons Virgo, it is a senseless waste of your intellect, your energy and your precious time.

If you leave demons in your
past, there is always a chance they
might come back to haunt you in the
present. If there is an issue or festering
hurt you still feel compelled to keep
picking over, now might be the time to
work through it and commit
to letting it go.

Moving forwards must be on your terms – to a place you are comfortable with, within a timeframe that works for you. Do not accept being rushed by someone else's plan.

Prosperity and wealth can
be measured in more than just
material possessions; count love, luck
and belonging among your
treasures Virgo.

Sinking into work is an excellent
(and typically Virgo) distraction
technique – it occupies your time and
your brainpower, leaving no room for
upsetting emotions to slink in and
startle you. But beware: if you ignore
them for too long, they will kick down
the door and insist that you
pay them some attention.

Be mindful of, and sensitive to, the feelings and egos of others. Diplomacy may feel frustrating, perhaps even disingenuous, at first, but you will reap greater long-term rewards if you tread carefully here.

Touch and physical contact are enormously important to you Virgo... as long as they are on your terms and under your direction. Massage, reflexology and energy work are all ideal stress-relievers, bringing both relief and rejuvenation.
Essential, really.

It can be an endless source of frustration to you Virgo, that others prefer politeness to truth and reality... But it is time to accept that that is just the way it is. Railing against their preference for soft focus and fairytales will only serve to exhaust your reserves and won't change those other people one little bit.

Others often perceive you to be a bit reserved, maybe even a cold fish, but what they don't understand is all the turmoil and emotion under the surface. Hiding it can seem essential, but you might consider sharing with someone you trust now and again.

Adopting an analytical approach to receiving feedback is the most logical and mature response, even if inside you are seething. The more you practice distancing your emotions from the process, the easier it will be next time round. Respond accordingly, then set it aside and carry on with your day. Once you've dealt with it, release it.

You are very happy to make sacrifices, work hard, commit yourself and persevere Virgo, but you need to be sure you are doing it for the right reasons. Is the exchange fair? Will you receive your due by return? If not, it might be time to make some changes.

Maintain that holding pattern for a little longer Virgo; it's not quite time yet, but your reward is on the way.

The more consideration you give the opinions of others, the more power you are allowing them to injure you. Don't give them that opportunity.

No matter how hard you engage
your thinking brain to wrestle with
the problem Virgo, there are some
outcomes you simply can't control.
Release your grip on this one – your
efforts are not having the
desired effect.

Random events can trigger the most unexpected (and unwelcome) emotions, leaving you drained or even unwell. Make some time to unwind – if you are less tightly coiled, everything will flow more smoothly.

Your impulse is to persist, to communicate and to worry at the issue until you make things right. But there is nothing more to be gained with this one and expending further effort will just result in more wasted energy. Time to back away.

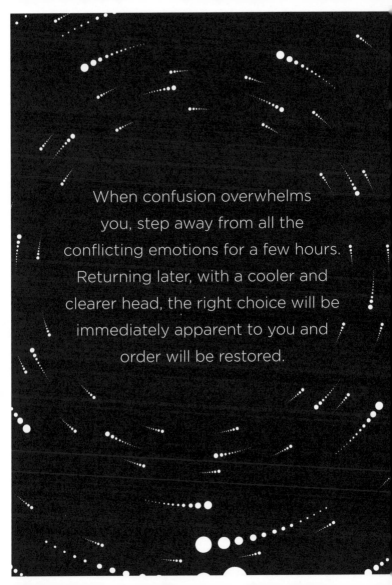

When confusion overwhelms you, step away from all the conflicting emotions for a few hours. Returning later, with a cooler and clearer head, the right choice will be immediately apparent to you and order will be restored.

Your emotions can feel rough and tangled Virgo, and this stimulates your tendency to prickliness, trying to keep others away from the parts that are easily hurt. If you can explain this, you might find a little more understanding than you anticipate.

A desire to escape and retreat is a typical Virgo trait, but one that sometimes you should resist. You have so much to contribute and braving the gaze of others is essential if you are to own your ideas. Push yourself. It will be worth it.

Comfortable or stuck Virgo?
Be honest – you owe it to yourself.
Once you answer this question, you
will know what needs to be done.

Break from your usual detail-oriented approach to answer this question Virgo. Take a big-picture view rather than focusing solely on the immediate issue; modify your expectations and be willing to adopt a much more flexible approach.

Your opinion is not always required... as much as you might be itching to give it. Taking the time to listen with warmth and patience is what's needed right now. You might even learn something about yourself in the process.

Although you might feel detached Virgo, your choices have implications for those around you. Obviously, you can't control everything that happens or have the foresight to anticipate all outcomes. But be sure you consider likely repercussions before you make a move that you won't be able to reverse.

Acknowledging your own needs,
and in a way that allows others to hear
them, is a skill you need to work at
continually Virgo – it does not come
naturally to you. Make sure that you
are receiving enough nourishment
to sustain you.

Although you may resent the redirection of your focus, it is important to ensure that others feel heard when they engage with you. Sometimes just your attention will be enough.

You often show a marked preference for the higher (rather than only the finer) things in life. You already know that acquisitions and material wealth are of no value in and of themselves – your best step right now would be to enrich your family and community in some way.

Time and patience will provide you
with the perspective you sorely need
at the moment Virgo. The temptation
to rush in is out of character for you
and will not be helpful in
the long-term.

With so many conflicting emotions and situations vying for your attention, things can become more than a little confused. It's not a feeling you enjoy Virgo, and the sensation of being sucked into a dizzying maelstrom can provoke a strongly negative response. Your best bet is to distract yourself with healthy and enjoyable pastimes until this stage passes.

Being under scrutiny is an unpleasant sensation for you at the best of times Virgo, and doubly so when it delivers criticism or judgement as well. Take the time to sit with your discomfort rather than running away, and don't take it personally.

Be mindful of your own force
when you are responding from a
place of pain Virgo. Lashing out
may temporarily relieve your own
frustration, but an impulsive urge to
share the hurt might cause unintended
collateral damage. Act quickly to
mop up whatever you can.

Adding a bit more focus to your practice, whether in your work or self-growth, will reap big rewards. Push the limits of your comfort zone Virgo – don't be too timid. And add a little self-love into the mix as well.

Playing it safe can sometimes wear you out Virgo, but creating memories isn't all about wild adventures. Create plans today and make something good happen. Something memorable.

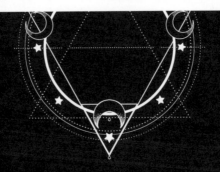

There may be increased energetic
undercurrents flowing through at
the moment Virgo. You are such an
intuitive sign, the emotional overloads
of others can weigh heavily on you
– do not underestimate the
impact this will have.

Time to pull everything back to the foundations Virgo. Find your feet again, get grounded and stand firmly in your place on the Earth.

Strange behaviour in others might not be as mysterious as it appears if you take the time to think more carefully about what has been going on. Focus on the basics.

Virgo endurance and determination are second to none, but your energy is a precious resource and shouldn't be squandered on an uncertain or flickering goal you are not completely sure of.

If you concentrate, make a plan and implement a strong and steady approach, you will certainly make amazing progress. Aim high and devote as much time as you can to achieving your dream.

When the right kind of energy is on your side, make the most of it by asking the questions you need answers to, and saying what you need to say so you can keep things moving.

Practical, reliable Virgos can sometimes surprise everyone by throwing it all up in the air and going wild. It doesn't happen often. And now is not one of those days. Reminiscing about past excitements might scratch the itch though – time to reconnect with a friend you shared some good times with.

Fresh new visuals will re-energize and inspire you Virgo. Make the most of your love for beautiful paintings, patterns, films, fabric and natural vistas; feast your eyes.

You might not be free to travel far right now Virgo, but there are plenty of adventures to be found closer to home.

If a particular relationship, past, present or perhaps even hoped-for, is occupying a large portion of your headspace right now, try to pull your attention back to the present moment a little more. You cannot control the outcome here; keep an open mind but carry on with your life.

When it feels like life is tumbling around you, perhaps moving faster than you are comfortable with, remember to look inwards to find the stillness; seek the beauty and happiness in the small things. Scaling it back for a while will help you restore your equilibrium.

Changing your mind is entirely allowable Virgo; you have no obligation to stick with a route you have now realized is heading in the wrong direction.

Sometimes it seems that you
can't settle on your own opinion!
Annoying as this can be for you (and
doubtless for others around you, too)
it is important to allow your
subconscious to bat this one back and
forth. You can be sure that the
decision you finally rest on
will be correct.

Narrowing down your choices is the best way to reach a final decision – perhaps you might need some help with this? Ask trusted friends their opinions, just not too many of them lest you end up with a whole new set of options to choose between.

If you need to retreat right now
Virgo, that's a perfectly valid response.
Just ensure that you use your time
wisely and well, doing something
enriching, rather than simply turning
away from the world.

Face up to any problems presenting themselves right now Virgo; heavy or unmanageable as they might feel, resist the urge to put them away for another time. Avoiding them will only ensure they come back trickier than ever, and meanwhile you will know they are lying in wait for you.

Stay awake to events Virgo, don't be tempted to shut yourself too tightly in an interior or escapist world right now. It is important to stay connected, to interact with your people and your surroundings, and to be informed.

Make the most of the days when
you feel strong, powerful and in
control Virgo. Blessings will flow.

Confusion and uncertainty may well result from frustrating situations and clashing energies at the moment. Others cannot understand how distracting and wearing you find all of this; it can feel like being trapped inside a thunder cloud as a storm rages. You will need to be mindful and introduce a little extra space around yourself.

When your energy is positive and your warmth radiates, there is nothing you cannot do Virgo. Those who might have previously found you reluctant to engage might be surprised at these different facets. Connect, but in a way that leaves room for adjustment without offence if you feel differently another time.

Finding yourself well-equipped to take advantage of favourable situations will happen more often and more easily if you leave some of your baggage at the door – you don't have to carry all of that around. Use the coat-check and take something off.

Enjoy the positivity when good vibes are resonating Virgo; make the most of what rises to the surface and reveals itself. There is no need to over-think anything right now.

Playing games is not really your style Virgo, don't be tempted into it this time – it won't end well. Take courage from how much you already know and speak out when the time is right. Until then, bide your time.

Holding your feelings in until they start to bite isn't healthy, but it is a very Virgo thing to do. Don't push your emotions down so hard that they have no outlet; inevitably that will lead to upsetting outcomes of one sort or another. Deal with issues as they arise.

When your physical and
emotional energy is high Virgo, there
is very little you can't achieve. On days
like this, get up and get going –
activity will help you get ahead and
feel less stressed about your
burgeoning to-do list.

Adversity often brings opportunity, but sometimes it just feels too much and you would rather give it all up. Try to take the long view and see past the immediate issue to what likely lies ahead. You don't need to plan every step along the way to get there.

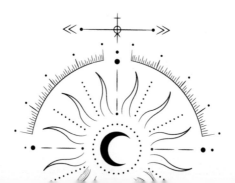

Your gut instinct was, unsurprisingly, correct. So often the way isn't it Virgo? Follow that famous intuition on this one; it will lead you in the right direction.

Escape into nature Virgo – you
need plenty of clean and positive
energy flowing around you if you are
to quickly replenish your recent
emotional drain.

When your social pool experiences ripples or upheaval it can throw you a little off-balance – for all your self-sufficiency, there are people you depend on. Don't be tempted to wade in with your opinion just for the sake of being involved, or make the mistake of trying to exert control. Be patient, calm will be restored again soon.

Change and turmoil can be frightening for some Virgo, but generally not for you. With a shake-up on the way, things might feel a little unpredictable for a while. Ride the wave.

New people can take a while to adjust to Virgo, and your natural suspicion of strangers may mean it takes you longer than others to find your place in a new group. Understand that others very likely feel exactly the same. Empathy is key right now.

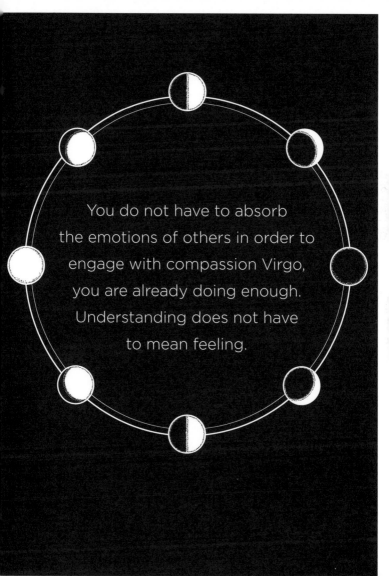

You do not have to absorb
the emotions of others in order to
engage with compassion Virgo,
you are already doing enough.
Understanding does not have
to mean feeling.

Don't allow second-guessing
your own judgement to overrule
your self-esteem Virgo.
Think, decide and act.

Underhand tactics just aren't your way, so it is always a shock to see others trying to manipulate situations and opinion to their own advantage. Maintain your distance and continue on your own path with integrity.

If others are easily convinced by
false information, is their opinion and
approval really so valuable?

While you might think you are being helpful, complaints are not necessarily the cleanest way to alert others to potential problems. Think carefully about how to phrase what you want to say and make it constructive.

Smaller groups or one-to-ones
are always your preference Virgo,
but if you find you can't avoid a large
gathering simply remind yourself that
it is made up of small groups. You
can travel between them, or
stick to just one.

Sometimes it feels like the world, or other people at least, don't have much to offer you. Don't allow that idea to take control, but think instead – what can you offer? Rather than retreating, find some way to engage – even a small one.

If you find you are struggling to
focus, check the weather forecast
and the moon phases... there may be
external pressures at play. Whatever
the reason, take time to rest
and recalibrate.

Your Virgo gifts of both intuition and almost alarmingly excellent memory make you a force to be reckoned with. Everyone has their own talents and you shouldn't give in to the urge to dial yours down just because you feel sorry for someone else. That won't help anyone.

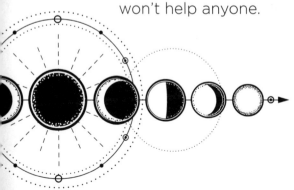

Linger in your own space Virgo –
holding your head together depends
on a certain amount of privacy and
downtime at the moment.

Make the effort to connect
with nurturing, non-demanding
friends right now Virgo. Even if you
haven't much time to spare, it will
be worth it.

A change of scenery might be just what you need Virgo – even a short trip out of town, an evening drive or a walk on a previously unexplored track. A small adjustment to your perspective may bring unexpectedly big rewards.

High drama may feel initially exciting, but often quickly tails off into simple disruption. Avoid the crisis-creators.

Crashing lows quite often follow those giddy highs Virgo. Instead of indulging, hold your balance and maintain an even keel. Don't get caught up in anyone else's freneticism – it's not your style.

While it can be a wonderful warm feeling to be wanted, it's time to re-balance some of those support-situations that seem to crop up so frequently. Always being the shoulder to cry on and the listening ear for a self-involved narcissist can get stale pretty fast.

Love should travel both ways
Virgo. If it's unrequited in either
direction, it's not working.

Fire can take hold quicker than
you expect Virgo. If you insist on
playing with it, keep a bucket of water
close by and be sure you know where
the exits are should you need to
make your escape.

Don't wade in too deep Virgo –
before you know it, you could be in
over your head. Keep dry land in sight.
And let someone else know that you
are going in.

If confidence is flowing for you
right now Virgo, make the most of it.
While you have some respite from
self-doubt, you will be able to see
much more clearly all you have
achieved and can feel proud of, and
where your potential really lies.

Especially on days when it feels
like anything might be possible, you
must make the most of opportunities
that come your way and store supplies
for the leaner times.

You are more than capable
of proving yourself worthy of
the trust others are placing
in you. Choose excitement
over anxiety Virgo.

If perfectionism is whispering
through the keyhole right now Virgo,
shove a tissue in there and turn up the
music. You need to get to the finish
line with this one, then, if there's time,
you can give it a polish.

Being highly visible can make
you feel vulnerable Virgo, especially if
you are standing alone in the spotlight.
Ask for support if you need it, but first
remind yourself how well prepared you
are and how much you already know.

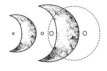

Don't let insecurity or over-thinking prevent you from stepping up Virgo. Projecting confidence, even if you don't quite feel it at the beginning, will get you halfway there.

If your intuition is sounding alarm bells about a partner or colleague right now, spend some time investigating. Is information being withheld or dishonesty at play somewhere along the line? Find a way to take a closer look...

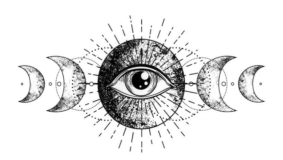

Don't allow your reliance on someone you don't trust to mean a missed opportunity for you Virgo. Find a way to work around them.

Working as part of a group isn't always the easiest for you Virgo, but make it manageable by keeping communication transparent and morale high. Don't be tempted to align yourself with one component over another unless that is a specific part of your role.

Keep everything easy and
buzzing Virgo. Carrying others along
with you is easier if you maintain good
vibes and momentum.

Unsolicited advice is not something you receive easily or happily Virgo. If there is some coming your way, try to work out whether it's spurred on by ego or whether it is a genuine attempt to help. Press pause on your instinctive bite-back.

Difficult as it is, it is essential you
apply some patience to this situation
Virgo, and give everything some time.

Awkward tension may arise quickly and surprisingly in your interactions Virgo; it is the price you pay for your highly-tuned intuition. Develop a strategy for gliding past rather than calling it out when it occurs, and nine times out of ten it will smooth over again in no time.

Bumps in the road are an inevitable part of the journey Virgo. Just hold tight to your map.

Chaos and mystery may reign
supreme at the moment Virgo; there is
little point trying to figure it all out. Try
to separate yourself so you can watch
from a distance... you might even find
some of it relatively amusing if you
no longer feel involved.

Self-sufficient as you are, it
can take a while to accept trust and
support without suspicion. If it is
offered with love, receive
it with love.

♈ ♉ ♊ ♋ ♌ ♍

Messy knots can take a long
time and a lot of work to untangle
Virgo – and it is essential to commit to
the task. Are you sure you have the
time and headspace available to
tackle this now?

Healing and repair don't
happen overnight Virgo. Rest,
good nourishment, clean air, positivity
and sunlight will all help.

If there is too much uncertainty to cope with alone, lean on those you trust. They will be flattered you chose them and pleased that they can repay all the times they have relied on you.

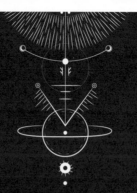

Indulging others' needs for attention and prolonged sympathy is never your strong point Virgo... but try to retain your patience and hear what is really being said. There may be valuable lessons beneath the words.

Truthful communication is a
strong point with you Virgos, but tact
and diplomacy can sometimes run a
little thin. Speak your truth but choose
the more diplomatic version.

Your strongly empathetic streak can present real difficulties when it comes to absorbing difficult energy from another source. Stick to provable facts right now Virgo, and stay open to changing your mind if you learn something new along the way.

Is your intuition telling you there
are avoidance techniques at play
Virgo? Trust your instinct.

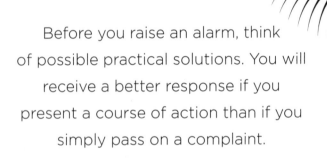

Before you raise an alarm, think of possible practical solutions. You will receive a better response if you present a course of action than if you simply pass on a complaint.

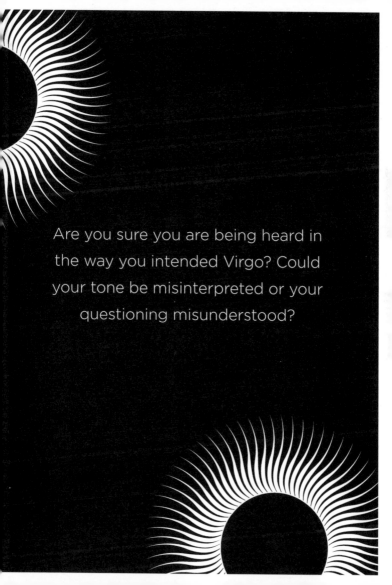

Are you sure you are being heard in the way you intended Virgo? Could your tone be misinterpreted or your questioning misunderstood?

Be sure you have your facts straight before you are drawn into a big blustering conversation about an important issue. Some people just wade in anyway, so strong is their desire to be seen and heard.
Don't be one of them.

Nourishment, brain food, rest and creative downtime are essential when energy and motivation seem to be flagging. Turning inwards will be hugely beneficial – you will feel restored in no time.

First published in Great Britain in 2021 by
Greenfinch
An imprint of Quercus Editions Ltd
Carmelite House
50 Victoria Embankment
London EC4Y 0DZ

An Hachette UK company

A CIP catalogue record for this book is available
from the British Library.

HB ISBN 978-1-52941-234-5

Every effort has been made to contact copyright holders.
However, the publishers will be glad to rectify in future editions any
inadvertent omissions brought to their attention.

10 9 8 7 6 5 4 3 2 1

Designed by Ginny Zeal
Cover design by Andrew Smith
Text by Susan Kelly
All images from Shutterstock.com

Printed and bound in China.

MIX
Paper from
responsible sources
FSC® C016973

Papers used by Greenfinch are from well-managed forests
and other responsible sources.